Carrousel Cards

Annelies Karduks

FORTE PUBLISHERS

Contents

ISBN 90 5877 452 x

This is a publication from
Forte Publishers BV
P.O. Box 1394
3500 BJ Utrecht
The Netherlands

For more information about the creative books available from Forte Uitgevers:
www.forteuitgevers.nl

Final editing: Gina Kors-Lambers, Steenwijk, the Netherlands
Photography and digital image editing: Fotografie Gerhard Witteveen, Apeldoorn, the Netherlands
Cover and inner design:
BADE creatieve communicatie, Baarn, the Netherlands
Translation: Michael Ford, TextCase, Hilversum, the Netherlands

Preface

I really enjoy designing new crafting products. This time, I have designed six square embossing templates. By rotating the embossing card, you can create different patterns each time. You can accentuate the patterns by cutting them or by using stamp-pad ink and fine-liners. Adding a 3D picture or a Rub-On picture produces a really attractive embossing card. Have fun discovering all the things you can do with the new Carré templates.

See page 32 if you wish to remain informed of what I have in store for you in the future.

Have fun.

Annelie

Techniques

It is important to always work accurately. Only then will the patterns join up nicely.

Embossing

Cut the embossing card to size (12 x 12 cm) and draw four squares (6 x 6 cm) on the back. Stick the Carré template on a light box. Place the corners of the square to be embossed level with the perpendicular corners in the template. Use template tape to stick the embossing card on the template and the light box with the good side facing downwards. Emboss (part of) the pattern by going over the lighted shapes with one of the embossing tools. Turn the card (or the template) a quarter of a revolution to create a mirror effect. If you wish, you can use Pergasoft to make the embossing easier.

Or

Cut the embossing card to size (13 x 13 cm). Draw four squares (6.5 x 6.5 cm) on the back of this embossing card. Place the perpendicular corner in the template level with the cross in the middle of the card and the opposite corner of the template level with the corner of the card. Next, emboss the card as described above.

Tip: Almost every square card measures 12 x 12 cm or 13 x 13 cm. If you use different colours of card, you will be left with pieces of these cards. You can use these pieces to make other cards.

Stamp-pad ink

Stamp-pad ink gives the best result when you emboss first. After embossing, turn the template and the embossing card over and place them on your work surface. Cover the parts which are not to be coloured with adhesive tape and stick the template down. It is best to stick the top and one side of the template to your work surface. Slide the embossing card in the correct position under the template and stick the template to the card. Apply stamp-pad ink to the sponge stick and dab or brush the pattern. If desired, use two colours to give it some depth. Lift the template using a finger nail and carefully remove the card. Rotate the card a quarter of a revolution and slide the card under the template again. Allow the stamp-pad ink to dry or speed up the drying process by heating the ink with a heat gun.

Cutting

Cutting gives the best result when you emboss first. After embossing, turn the template and the embossing card over and place them on your work surface. Stick the template to the embossing card. Hold a sharp knife vertically

1. Embossing and rotating the embossing card.

2. Adding stamp-pad ink.

3. Using a template to cut the paper.

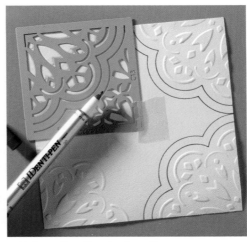

4. Using a fine-liner to draw lines.

*Pattern B: Butterflies
Increase in size by 143%*

*Pattern A: Red Christmas
Increase in size by 143%*

and cut the lines in the template. Always cut along the same side of the cutting line. If desired, mark each part, so that you stick them back on the card in the correct order. For a square measuring 13 x 13 cm, place the outer corner of the template level with the corner of the square and stick the template down. Next, cut the card as described above. The outer cutting line is the line furthest away from the middle of the square. The inner cutting line is the line nearest to the middle of the square.

Fine-liner

Place the embossed card on your work surface with the template on top and stick the template to the embossing card. Use a suitable colour to draw the lines in the Carré template, making sure to draw the line in one go.

Using tape

Use template tape from Kars when embossing Mi-Teintes card. This tape has a glue layer which is able to withstand the heat from a light box. This tape is also good to use when sticking the template to your work surface. However, if

you must stick adhesive tape to the good side of the embossing card (when dabbing stamp-pad ink, when cutting the cutting lines and when using fine-liners to draw the lines), use 3M Scotch Removable Magic Tape. This tape has a glue layer which is not as sticky as the tape described above and is easier to remove from the embossing card. Also use this tape when embossing cArt-us card. Use a new piece of tape for every card and save the used pieces of tape to cover the unused parts of the template when applying the stamp-pad ink.

Materials

- ❏ Card and paper: cArt-us (CA), Mi-Teintes Canson (C) and Papicolor (P) (the number is stated for every type of card)
- ❏ Carré templates: C01, C02, C03, C11, C12 and C13
- ❏ Scoring pen
- ❏ Cutting ruler with a metal edge
- ❏ Cutting mat
- ❏ Hobby knife
- ❏ Tweezer scissors

- ❏ Template tape
- ❏ 3M Scotch Removable Magic Tape
- ❏ 3D cutting sheets
- ❏ Rub-On pictures
- ❏ Photo glue
- ❏ 3D foam tape/blocks of foam tape and/or 3D glue
- ❏ Light box
- ❏ Fiskars embossing tool (small tip)
- ❏ Fiskars embossing tool (regular tip)

- ❏ Eyelets
- ❏ Eyelet tool
- ❏ Eyelet hammer
- ❏ Needle
- ❏ Propelling pencil
- ❏ Rubber
- ❏ Pritt On & Off
- ❏ Stamp-pad petal point: 8-colour pinwheel
- ❏ Stamp-pad paintbox: 12 pastel colours
- ❏ Sponge sticks
- ❏ Heat gun

Card with robin redbreasts *(see title page)*

What you need
- ❏ Card: orange C453 (P11) and white C335 (P30)
- ❏ Carré embossing template C03
- ❏ Step-by-step cutting sheet: Hellebores IT 0406
- ❏ Stamp-pad ink: orange

Cut, score and fold a white double card (13.5 x 13.5 cm). Cut a white square (12 x 12 cm) and an orange square (13 x 13 cm). Look at the photograph at the front of the book to see which part of the pattern has been left out and how the square must be placed on the template. Emboss the pattern four times as described in Techniques. Apply orange stamp-pad ink to all the embossed parts and allow it to dry. Stick the template on the front of the embossed square and cut both cutting lines. Do this four times. Stick the orange square and the five parts on the card. Use 3D glue to stick the robin redbreasts on the card.

Purple flowers

Card 1

What you need
❏ Card:
dark blue
CA417 (P41),
violet CA425
(P20) and white
C335 (P30)
❏ Carré
embossing
template C13
❏ Cutting sheets:
3x Picturel Spring flowers (no. 540)

Cut, score and fold a violet double card (13.5 x 13.5 cm). Cut a dark blue square (13 x 13 cm) and a white square (13 x 13 cm). Look at the photograph to see which part of the pattern has been left out and how the white square must be placed on the template. Emboss the pattern four times as described in Techniques. Stick the template on the front of the embossed square and cut the inner cutting line. Do this four times. Stick the template on the dark blue square as described in Techniques and cut both cutting lines. Do this four times. Cut the corners out of the frame 0.5 cm from the edge. Stick the frame and the white cross on the card. Make the picture 3D.

Card 2

What you need
❏ Card: dark blue CA417 (P41),
violet CA425 (P20) and white C335 (P30)
❏ Carré embossing template C03
❏ Cutting sheets:
4x Picturel Spring flowers (no. 540)

Cut, score and fold a dark blue double card (13.5 x 13.5 cm). Cut four white squares (6 x 6 cm) and four violet squares (6.5 x 6.5 cm). Look at the photograph to see which part of the pattern has been left out and how the white square must be placed on the template. Place the square level with the perpendicular corners in the template. Emboss the pattern twice as described in Techniques. Also emboss the cutting lines. Do this for all the white squares. Stick the squares on the card. Use 3D glue to stick the flowers on the card.

Card 3

What you need
❏ Card: dark blue CA417 (P41),
violet CA425 (P20) and white C335 (P30)
❏ Carré embossing template C01
❏ Cutting sheets:
3x Picturel Spring flowers (no. 540)
❏ Stamp-pad ink: heliotrope and royal blue

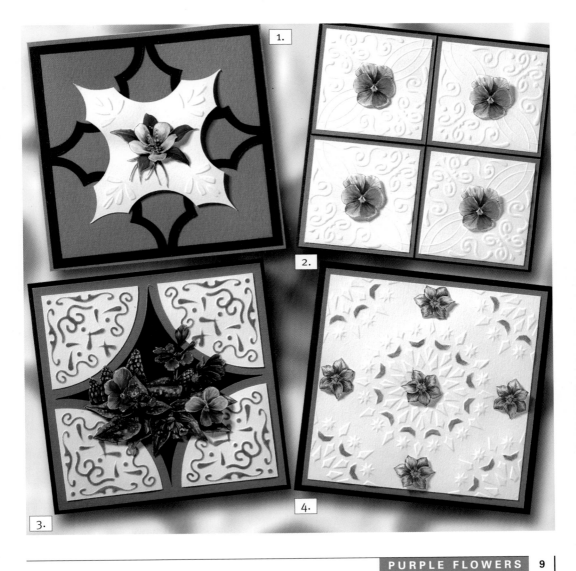

1.

2.

3.

4.

Cut, score and fold a dark blue double card (13.5 x 13.5 cm). Cut a violet square (13 x 13 cm) and a white square (12 x 12 cm). Look at the photograph to see which part of the pattern has been left out and how the white square must be placed on the template. Emboss the pattern four times as described in Techniques. Apply both colours of stamp-pad ink to the embossed parts and allow it to dry. Stick the template on the front of the embossed square and cut the outer cutting line. Do this four times. Stick the template on the violet square as described in Techniques and cut the inner cutting line. Do this four times. Stick the five parts on the card. Make the picture 3D.

Card 4

What you need

❏ *Card: dark blue CA417 (P41),*
violet CA425 (P20) and white C335 (P30)
❏ *Carré embossing template C11*
❏ *Cutting sheets:*
5x Picturel Spring flowers (no. 540)
❏ *Stamp-pad ink: heliotrope and royal blue*

Cut, score and fold a dark blue double card (13.5 x 13.5 cm). Cut a violet square (12.7 x 12.7 cm) and a white square (12 x 12 cm). Look at the photograph to see which part of the pattern has been left out and how the white square must be placed on the template. Emboss the pattern eight times as described in Techniques. Apply both colours of stamp-pad ink to some of the embossed parts and allow it to dry. Stick the squares on the card. Use 3D glue to stick the flowers on the card.

Butterflies

Card 1

What you need
- ❏ Card: natural CA211 (P03), high yellow C400 (P10) and orange C453 (P11)
- ❏ Carré embossing template C13
- ❏ Step-by-step cutting sheet: Hydrangea IT 0407
- ❏ Stamp-pad ink: orange

Cut, score and fold a natural double card (13.5 x 13.5 cm). Cut a yellow square (12 x 12 cm), a natural square (12 x 12 cm) and an orange square (12.7 x 12.7 cm). Look at the photograph to see which part of the pattern has been left out and how the yellow square must be placed on the template. Emboss the pattern four times as described in Techniques. Apply orange stamp-pad ink to the embossed parts and allow it to dry. Stick the template on the front of the embossed square and cut the inner cutting lines. Do this four times. Stick the squares and the flower on the card. Use 3D glue to stick the butterflies on the card.

Card 2

What you need
- ❏ Card: natural CA211 (P03), terracotta CA549 (P35), high yellow C400 (P10) and orange C453 (P11)
- ❏ Carré embossing template C12

- ❏ Step-by-step cutting sheet: Pink roses IT no. 400
- ❏ Stamp-pad ink: orange

Cut, score and fold a natural double card (10.5 x 14.8 cm). Cut two yellow squares (6 x 6 cm) and two terracotta squares (6.5 x 6.5 cm). Look at the photograph to see which part of the pattern has been left out and how the yellow square must be placed on the template. Place the square level with the perpendicular corners in the template. Emboss the pattern twice as described in Techniques. Repeat this for the other yellow square. Apply orange stamp-pad ink to the embossed parts and allow it to dry. Cut two 1 cm wide orange strips. Stick the strips and the squares on the card. Use 3D glue to stick the butterflies on the card.

Card 3

What you need
- ❏ *Card: natural CA211 (P03) and*
  terracotta CA549 (P35)
- ❏ *Carré embossing template C01*
- ❏ *Rub-On large butterflies*
- ❏ *Stamp-pad ink: orange*

Cut, score and fold a natural double card (13.5 x 13.5 cm). Cut a terracotta square (13 x 13 cm) and a natural square (12.5 x 12.5 cm). Look at the photograph to see which part of the pattern has been left out and how the natural square must be placed on the template. Emboss the pattern four times as described in Techniques keeping the perpendicular corner in the template level with the cross in the middle. Apply orange stamp-pad ink to the embossed parts and allow it to dry. Stick the squares on the card. Copy pattern B and carefully cut it out. Use Pritt On & Off to stick it on the card. Punch holes and attach eyelets to the card. Rub the butterfly on the card.

Card 4

What you need
- ❏ *Card: natural CA211 (P03), ochre CA575*
  and high yellow C400 (P10)
- ❏ *Carré embossing template C03*
- ❏ *Step-by-step cutting sheet:*
  Yellow roses IT no. 399
- ❏ *Metallic fun eyelet shapes (gold)*

Cut, score and fold an ochre double card (13.5 x 13.5 cm). Cut a yellow square (12.7 x 12.7 cm) and a natural square (12 x 12 cm). Look at the photograph to see which part of the pattern has been left out and how the natural square must be placed on the template. Emboss the pattern eight times as described in Techniques. Stick the squares on the card and attach the eyelet shapes. Use 3D glue to stick the butterflies on the card.

Sunflowers

Card 1

What you need
- ❏ Card: golden yellow CA247 (P10), black CA219 (P01), spring green CA305 (P08) and white C335 (P30)
- ❏ Carré embossing template C03
- ❏ Step-by-step cutting sheet: Sunflowers IT 0408

Cut, score and fold a yellow double card (13.5 x 13.5 cm). Cut a white square (12 x 12 cm), a green square (12 x 12 cm) and a black square (13 x 13 cm). Look at the photograph to see which part of the pattern has been left out and how the white square and the green square must be placed on the template. Emboss the pattern four times as described in Techniques on both squares. Stick the template on the front of the embossed squares and cut both cutting lines. Do this four times. Stick the black square and the five parts on the card. Make the picture 3D.

Card 2

What you need
- ❏ Card: black CA219 (P01), spring green CA305 (P08) and white C335 (P30)
- ❏ Carré embossing template C11
- ❏ Step-by-step cutting sheet: Sunflowers IT 0408

Cut, score and fold a black double card (13.5 x 13.5 cm). Cut a white square (13 x 13 cm) and a green square (13 x 13 cm). Look at the photograph to see which part of the pattern has been left out and how the white square must be placed on the template. Emboss the pattern four times as described in Techniques. Stick the template on the front of the embossed square and cut the inner cutting lines. Do this four times. Stick the template on the green square as described in Techniques and cut both cutting lines. Do this four times. Cut the corners out of the square 0.5 cm from the edge. Stick the frame and the white flower on the card. Make the picture 3D.

Card 3

What you need
- ❏ Card: black CA219 (P01), spring green CA305 (P08) and white C335 (P30)
- ❏ Carré embossing template C01
- ❏ Step-by-step cutting sheet: Sunflowers IT 0408
- ❏ Stamp-pad ink: canary
- ❏ Black fine-liner

Cut, score and fold a black double card (13.5 x 13.5 cm). Cut a white square (12 x 12 cm), a green square (12.7 x 12.7 cm) and a black square (13 x 13 cm). Look at the photograph to see which part of the pattern has been left out and how the white square must be placed on the template. Emboss the pattern four times as described in Techniques. Apply canary stamp-pad ink to all the embossed parts and allow it to dry. Stick the template on the front of the embossed square and use the fine-liner to draw the outer cutting line. Do this four times. Stick the template on the black square as described in Techniques and cut the inner cutting line. Do this four times. Stick the squares and the diamond on the card. Make the picture 3D.

Card 4

What you need
❑ *Card: black CA219 (P01), spring green CA305 (P08) and white C335 (P30)*
❑ *Carré embossing template C02*
❑ *Step-by-step cutting sheet: Sunflowers IT 0408*
❑ *Stamp-pad ink: lime*
❑ *Black fine-liner*
❑ *Mini eyelet rings (silver)*

Cut, score and fold a green double card (13.5 x 13.5 cm). Cut a white square (12 x 12 cm) and a black square (12.7 x 12.7 cm). Look at the photograph to see which part of the pattern has been left out and how the white square must be placed on the template. Emboss the pattern four times as described in Techniques. Apply lime stamp-pad ink to the inner embossed parts and allow it to dry. Stick the template on the front of the embossed square and use the fine-liner to draw both cutting lines. Do this four times. Stick the squares on the card and attach the eyelets. Make the picture 3D.

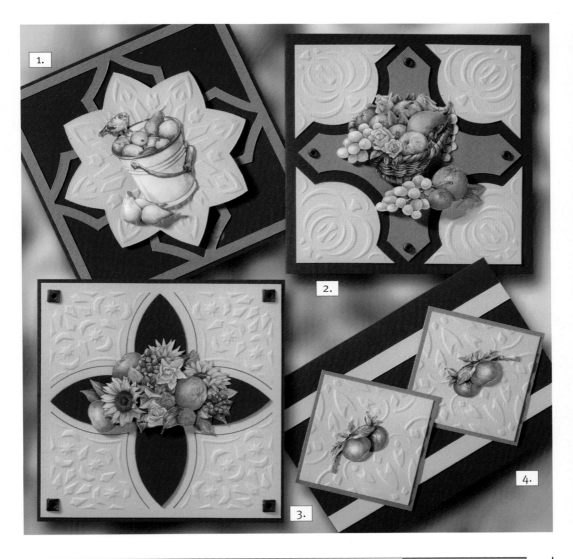

Fruit

Card 1

What you need
- ❏ *Card: dark red CA519 (P43), golden yellow CA247 (P10) and apple green C475 (P169)*
- ❏ *Carré embossing template C12*
- ❏ *Picturel Cutting sheets:*
  3x Fruit decorations no. 548

Cut, score and fold a dark red double card (13.5 x 13.5 cm). Cut a yellow square (13 x 13 cm) and a green square (13 x 13 cm). Look at the photograph to see which part of the pattern has been left out and how the yellow square must be placed on the template. Emboss the pattern four times as described in Techniques. Stick the template on the front of the embossed square and cut the inner cutting line. Do this four times. Stick the template on the green card as described in Techniques (the template is rotated 180 degrees compared to the yellow square) and cut both cutting lines. Do this four times. Cut the corners out of the frame 0.5 cm from the edge. Stick the frame and the yellow flower on the card. Make the picture 3D.

Card 2

What you need
- ❏ *Card: dark red CA519 (P43), golden yellow CA247 (P10) and apple green C475 (P169)*
- ❏ *Carré embossing template C02*
- ❏ *Picturel Cutting sheets:*
  3x Get well soon bear no. 549
- ❏ *Metallic fun eyelet shapes (red)*

Cut, score and fold a dark red double card (13.5 x 13.5 cm). Cut a green square (13 x 13 cm) and a yellow square (12 x 12 cm). Look at the photograph to see which part of the pattern has been left out and how the yellow square must be placed on the template. Emboss the pattern four times as described in Techniques. Stick the template on the front of the embossed square and cut the outer cutting line. Do this four times. Stick the template on the green square as described in Techniques and cut the inner cutting line. Do this four times. Stick the five parts on the card and attach the eyelets. Make the picture 3D.

Card 3

What you need
- ❏ *Card: dark red CA519 (P43) and*
  golden yellow CA247 (P10)
- ❏ *Carré embossing template C11*
- ❏ *Picturel Cutting sheets:*
  3x Get well soon bear no. 549
- ❏ *Metallic fun eyelet shapes (red)*
- ❏ *Red fine-liner*

Cut, score and fold a dark red double card (13.5 x 13.5 cm). Cut a yellow square (13 x 13 cm) and a red square (13 x 13 cm). Look at the photograph to see which part of the pattern has been left out and how the yellow square must be placed on the template. Emboss the pattern four times as described in Techniques. Stick the template on the front of the embossed square and use the fine-liner to draw the outer cutting line. Do this four times. Stick the template on the red square as described in Techniques and cut the inner cutting line. Do this four times. Stick the yellow square and the red shape on the card. Attach the eyelets. Make the picture 3D.

Card 4

What you need
- ❏ *Card: dark red CA519 (P43), golden yellow*
  CA247 (P10) and apple green C475 (P169)
- ❏ *Carré embossing template C13*
- ❏ *Picturel Cutting sheets:*
  2x Fruit decorations no. 548

Cut, score and fold a dark red double card (10.5 x 14.8 cm). Cut two yellow squares (6 x 6 cm) and two green squares (6.5 x 6.5 cm). Look at the photograph to see which part of the pattern has been left out and how the yellow square must be placed on the template. Place the square level with the perpendicular corners in the template. Emboss the pattern twice as described in Techniques. Do this for both yellow squares. Cut two 1 cm wide yellow strips. Stick the strips and the squares on the card. Make the apples 3D.

Flowers

Card 1

What you need:
- ❏ *Card: aquamarine CA427 (P06),*
  light blue CA391 (P42) and white C335 (P30)
- ❏ *Carré embossing template C03*
- ❏ *Eline cutting sheet: Spring flowers AK 1007*
- ❏ *Stamp-pad ink: sky blue and royal blue*

Cut, score and fold an aquamarine double card (13.5 x 13.5 cm). Cut a light blue square (13 x 13 cm) and a white square (12 x 12 cm). Look at the photograph to see which part of the pattern has been left out and how the white square must be placed on the template. Emboss the pattern four times as described in Techniques. Apply both colours of stamp-pad ink to the embossed parts and allow the ink to dry. Stick the template on the front of the embossed square and cut the outer cutting line. Do this four times. Stick the template on the light blue square as described in Techniques and cut the inner cutting line. Do this four times. Stick the five parts on the card. Use foam tape or 3D glue to stick the picture on the card.

Card 2

What you need:
- ❏ *Card: dark red CA519 (P43), pink CA481 (P34)*
  and white C335 (P30)
- ❏ *Carré embossing template C01*
- ❏ *Eline cutting sheet: Four-leaf clover AK 1009*

Cut, score and fold a pink double card (13.5 x 13.5 cm). Cut four white squares (6 x 6 cm) and four dark red squares (6.5 x 6.5 cm). Look at the photograph to see which part of the pattern has been left out and how the white square must be placed on the template. Place the square level with the perpendicular corners in the template. Emboss the pattern twice as described in Techniques. Also emboss one cutting line. Do this for all the white squares. Stick the squares on the card. Use foam tape or 3D glue to stick the flowers on dark red squares (2 x 2 cm) and use foam tape or 3D glue to stick them on the card.

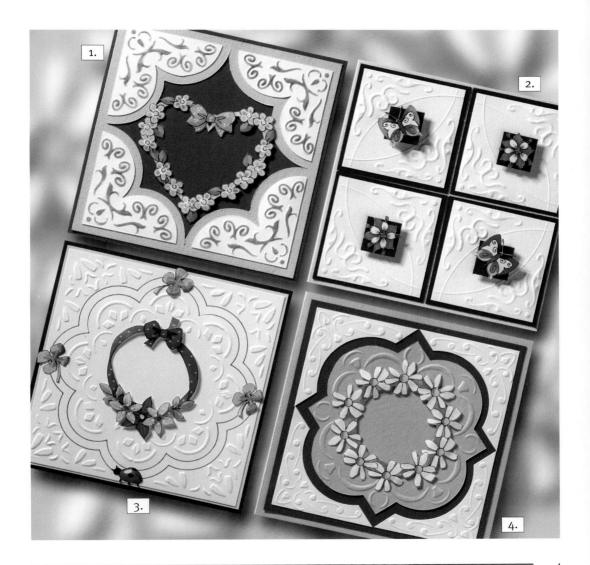

1.

2.

3.

4.

Card 3

What you need:

- ❏ Card: dark red CA519 (P43), pink CA481 (P34) and white C335 (P30)
- ❏ Carré embossing template C13
- ❏ Eline cutting sheet: Four-leaf clover AK 1009
- ❏ Dark red fine-liner

Cut, score and fold a dark red double card (13.5 x 13.5 cm). Cut a pink square (13 x 13 cm) and a white square (13 x 13 cm). Look at the photograph to see which part of the pattern has been left out and how the white square must be placed on the template. Emboss the pattern four times as described in Techniques. Stick the template on the front of the embossed square and use the fine-liner to draw both cutting lines. Do this four times. Cut the white square so that it measures 12.5 x 12.5 cm. Stick the squares on the card. Use foam tape or 3D glue to stick the middle picture on the card and use photo glue to stick the other pictures on the card.

Card 4

What you need:

- ❏ Card: aquamarine CA427 (P06), light blue CA391 (P42) and white C335 (P30)
- ❏ Carré embossing template C02
- ❏ Eline cutting sheet: Spring flowers AK 1007

Cut, score and fold a light blue double card (13.5 x 13.5 cm). Cut an aquamarine square (12.7 x 12.7 cm), a light blue square (13 x 13 cm) and a white square (12 x 12 cm). Look at the photograph to see which part of the pattern has been left out and how the white square and the light blue square must be placed on the template. Emboss the pattern four times as described in Techniques. Stick the template on the front of the embossed squares and cut both cutting lines. Do this four times. Stick the aquamarine square and the five parts on the card. Use foam tape or 3D glue to stick the picture on the card.

Green Christmas

Card 1

What you need:
- ❏ *Card: dark green CA309 (P18),*
  apple green C475 (P169) and lemon C101 (P29)
- ❏ *Carré embossing template C11*
- ❏ *Marjoleine cutting sheet:*
  Green Christmas decorations
- ❏ *Metallic fun eyelet shapes (green)*

Cut, score and fold a dark green double card
(13.5 x 13.5 cm). Cut two lemon squares (12.7 x
12.7 cm and 9 x 9 cm) and an apple green
square (9.5 x 9.5 cm). Look at the photograph to
see which part of the pattern has been left out
and how the square must be placed on the template. Emboss both lemon squares by placing
the corners level with the perpendicular corner
in the template so that the embossing comes
right up to the edge of the squares. Attach the
eyelets. Make the Christmas decorations 3D.

Card 2

What you need:
- ❏ *Card: dark green CA309 (P18),*
  apple green C475 (P169) and lemon C101 (P29)
- ❏ *Carré embossing template C12*
- ❏ *Step-by-step cutting sheet:*
  Candles MD no. 433
- ❏ *Metallic fun eyelet shapes (green)*

- ❏ *Adhesive stones: brown 4 mm*
- ❏ *Scribbles glittering crystal*

Cut, score and fold a dark green double card
(13.5 x 13.5 cm). Cut a lemon square (12 x 12 cm)
and an apple green square (12.7 x 12.7 cm).
Look at the photograph to see which part of the
pattern has been left out and how the square
must be placed on the template. Emboss the
pattern four times as described in Techniques.
Also emboss the cutting lines. Stick the squares
on the card. Punch eyelets in the card and use
Scribbles to stick the adhesive stones on the
card. Make the Christmas candles 3D.

Card 3

What you need:

❑ *Card: dark green CA309 (P18),*
apple green C475 (P169) and lemon C101 (P29)
❑ *Carré embossing template C02*
❑ *Step-by-step cutting sheet:*
Candles MD no. 433
❑ *Adhesive stones: brown 4 mm*
❑ *Scribbles glittering crystal*

Cut, score and fold a dark green double card
(13.5 x 13.5 cm). Cut one lemon square (12 x
12 cm) and two apple green squares (13 x 13 cm).
Look at the photograph to see which part of the
pattern has been left out and how the square
must be placed on the template. Emboss the
pattern four times as described in Techniques.
Stick the template on the front a green square
as described in Techniques and cut both cutting
lines. Do this four times. Increase the length
of the cutting lines to cut out the frame. Stick
the squares and the frame on the card. Use
Scribbles to stick the adhesive stones on the
card. Make the Christmas candles 3D.

Card 4

What you need:

❑ *Card: dark green CA309 (P18),*
apple green C475 (P169) and lemon C101 (P29)
❑ *Carré embossing template C01*
❑ *Marjoleine cutting sheet:*
Green Christmas decorations

Cut, score and fold a dark green double card
(13.5 x 13.5 cm). Cut four lemon squares (6 x
6 cm) and an apple green square (13 x 13 cm).
Look at the photograph to see which part of the
pattern has been left out and how the lemon
square must be placed on the template. Place
the square level with the perpendicular corners
in the template. Emboss the pattern twice
as described in Techniques. Also emboss the
cutting lines. Do this for all the lemon squares.
Stick the squares on the card. Make the
Christmas decorations 3D.

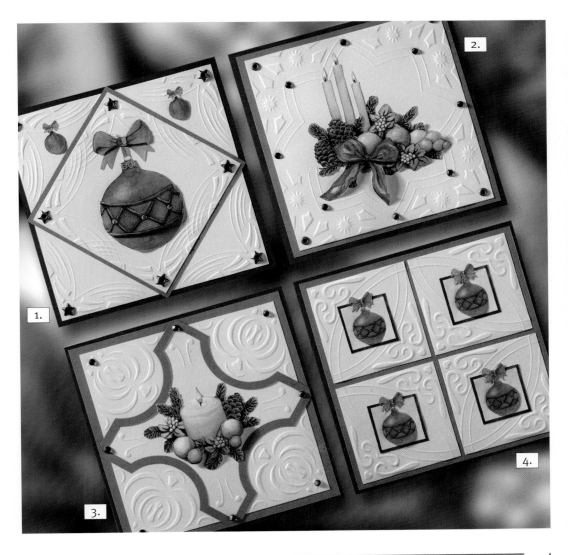

1.

2.

3.

4.

Snow

Card 1

What you need:
- ❏ *Card: white CA210 (P30),*
  dark blue CA417 (P41)
  and azure C102 (P42)
- ❏ *Carré embossing template C03*
- ❏ *Rub-On snowmen/snowballs*
- ❏ *Transparent paper elements*

Cut, score and fold a white double card (13.5 x 13.5 cm). Cut a dark blue square (13 x 13 cm), a transparent square (12.5 x 12.5 cm) and an azure square (13 x 13 cm). Look at the photograph to see which part of the pattern has been left out and how the azure square must be placed on the template. Emboss the pattern four times as described in Techniques. Stick the template on the front of the embossed square and cut the inner cutting lines. Do this four times. Make the dark blue square into a 1.5 cm wide frame. Stick the transparent square, the frame and the azure shape on the card. Rub the snowman and the snow crystals on the card.

Card 2

What you need:
- ❏ *Card: cornflower blue CA393 (P05),*
  dark blue CA417 (P41) and azure C102 (P42)
- ❏ *Carré embossing template C13*
- ❏ *Rub-On snowmen/snowballs*
- ❏ *Stamp-pad ink: lavender and aqua*

Cut, score and fold a cornflower blue double card (13.5 x 13.5 cm). Cut an azure square (12 x 12 cm) and a dark blue square (12.5 x 12.5 cm). Look at the photograph to see which part of the pattern has been left out and how the azure square must be placed on the template. Emboss the pattern four times as described in Techniques. Apply both colours of stamp-pad ink to the embossed parts and allow the glue to dry. Stick the template on the front of the embossed square and cut both cutting lines. Do this four times. Stick the square and the five parts on the card. Rub the snowman on the card.

Card 3

What you need:
- ❏ *Card: cornflower blue CA393 (P05),*
  dark blue CA417 (P41) and azure C102 (P42)
- ❏ *Carré embossing template C02*
- ❏ *Rub-On snowmen/snowballs*
- ❏ *Stamp-pad ink: lavender and aqua*

Cut, score and fold a dark blue double card (13.5 x 13.5 cm). Cut a cornflower blue square (13 x 13 cm), two azure squares (12 x 12 cm and 8 x 8 cm) and a dark blue square (8.5 x 8.5 cm). Look at the photograph to see which part of the pattern has been left out and how the square must be placed on the template. Emboss both azure squares by placing the corners level with the perpendicular corner in the template. Apply both colours of stamp-pad ink to the embossed parts and allow the glue to dry. Stick the squares on the card. Rub the snowman and the snow stars on the card.

Card 4

What you need:
- ❏ *Card: white CA210 (P30), dark blue CA417 (P41) and azure C102 (P42)*
- ❏ *Carré embossing template C12*
- ❏ *Rub-On snowmen/snowballs*
- ❏ *Transparent paper elements*
- ❏ *Decoration chalks*

Cut, score and fold a white double card (13.5 x 13.5 cm). Cut a dark blue square (13 x 13 cm), a transparent square (12.5 x 12.5 cm) and an azure square (13 x 13 cm). Look at the photograph to see which part of the pattern has been left out and how the azure square must be placed on the template. Emboss the pattern four times as described in Techniques. Stick the template on the front of the embossed square and cut the inner cutting lines. Do this four times. Use chalk to decorate the edges. Stick the template on the dark blue square as described in Techniques and cut both cutting lines. Do this four times. Cut the corners out of the frame 0.5 cm from the edge. Rub the sign with text onto the cross. Stick the transparent square, the frame and the cross on the card.

1.

2.

3.

4.

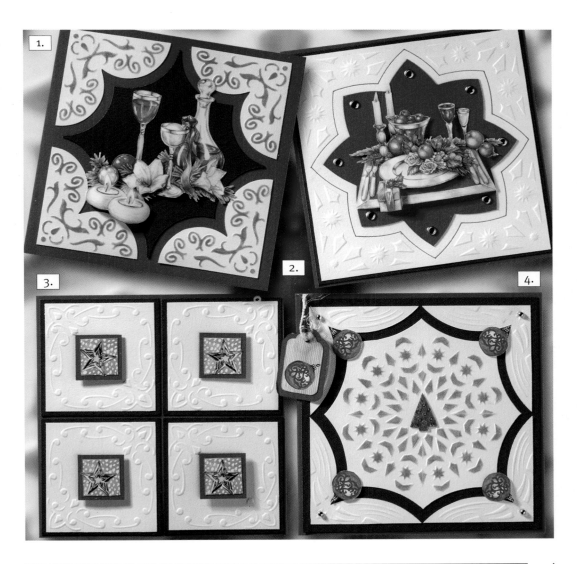

Red Christmas

Card 1

What you need:

- ❏ Card: old red CA517 (P12), dark green CA309 (P18) and white C335 (P30)
- ❏ Carré embossing template C03
- ❏ Cutting sheets: 3x Picturel Christmas dinner (no. 552)
- ❏ Stamp-pad ink: scarlet

Cut, score and fold a red double card (13.5 x 13.5 cm). Cut a white square (12 x 12 cm) and a dark green square (13 x 13 cm). Look at the photograph to see which part of the pattern has been left out and how the white square must be placed on the template. Emboss the pattern four times as described in Techniques. Apply scarlet stamp-pad ink to all the embossed parts and allow it to dry. Stick the template on the front of the embossed square and cut both cutting lines. Do this four times. Stick the template on the green square as described in Techniques and cut the inner cutting line. Do this four times. Stick the five parts on the card. Make the picture 3D.

Card 2

What you need:

- ❏ Card: old red CA517 (P12), dark green CA309 (P18) and white C335 (P30)
- ❏ Carré embossing template C12
- ❏ Cutting sheets: 3x Picturel Christmas dinner (no. 552)
- ❏ Mine eyelet rings (gold)
- ❏ Red fine-liner

Cut, score and fold a red double card (13.5 x 13.5 cm). Cut a white square (13 x 13 cm), a red square (13 x 13 cm) and a dark green square (13 x 13 cm). Look at the photograph to see which part of the pattern has been left out and how the white square must be placed on the template. Emboss the pattern four times as described in Techniques. Stick the template on the front of the embossed square and use the fine-liner to draw the outer cutting line. Do this four times. Cut 2.5 mm off every side of the white square. Stick the template on the front of the red square as described in Techniques and cut the inner cutting line. Do this four times. Stick the squares and the star on the card. Copy pattern A and carefully cut it out. Use Pritt On & Off to stick it on the red star. Punch holes for the eyelets and add the eyelets. Make the picture 3D.